Parkinson's is a progressive neurological condition for which there is currently no cure. The condition develops when nerve cells that are responsible for producing a chemical known as dopamine die. Dopamine allows messages to be sent to the parts of the brain that coordinate movement. With the loss of dopamine-producing nerve cells, these parts of the brain are unable to work normally, causing symptoms of Parkinson's to appear.

There are more than 40 symptoms of the condition. As well as the most widely known symptom - tremor - these range from physical symptoms like muscle stiffness to depression, anxiety, hallucinations, memory problems and dementia - but Parkinson's affects everyone differently. Parkinson's doesn't directly cause people to die, but symptoms do get worse over time.

In the UK, around 153,000 people are already living with Parkinson's. With population growth and ageing, we estimate that this will increase to around 172,000 people in the UK by 2030. There is currently no cure for Parkinson's, but there are lots of different treatments, therapies and support available to help manage the condition.

There is scientific proof that poetry along with other forms of art is an effective therapy especially for managing mental health. People who develop Parkinsons often experience a surge in creativity even where none apparently existed before, while practised writers and artists frequently report a renewed creative urge and heightening of their talents while living with the condition.

For more information on living with Parkinson's, the latest research and how you can help visit www. parkinsons.org.uk

Words from the Wall

Dedicated to everyone affected by Parkinson's including those living with the condition, their families and friends

copyright @ 2024 by poetswall.com

All rights reserved.
No parts of this book may be reproduced in any manner without written permission except in the case of brief quotations included in critical articles and reviews.

ISBN: 9798322484028

Published by- Denton Business Services Ltd.

Editing Team

Alison Blevins
Martin Pickard
Nigel Smith
Dawson Stafford

Designed by - Dawson Stafford

Foreword

Welcome to 'Words from the Wall', the first poetry anthology written by members of the collective known as 'Poets with Parkinson's'. Our home is 'the Wall', and its purpose is to provide a safe, peaceful and encouraging place for anyone touched by Parkinson's. We nurture and improve our Art by interacting with other members in friendship at The Wall, and 'Open Mic' sessions.

Poetry, Peace, and the Positive.

Nigel Smith - Co Founder

Contents

		Page
Jon Best	Melted Memories	3
	Cruel	4
	The Grumblebug	5
Katharina Beyer	Everywhere	7
	What I Believe	8
	Yorkshire Rose	9
Tincy Binu	Be a Parkinson	11
	Together Apart	12-13
Alison Blevins	Self Portrait	15
	Some Days	16
	I Lie to You at Least Twice a Day	17
Valerie Bowden	Parkinson's Awareness	19-20
	Locked Away	21
Jarlath Busby	A Winters Tail	23
	Parkinson's Reveille	24
	Distant Planets	25
	Drop of Hope	25
Luisa Candela	Dark Inside	27
	Music in the Dawn	28
	Living Anyway	29
Alice Carroll	My Parkie Bizzaro World of Dreams	31
	Unidentified	32
	Downsize	33
Debbie Dalton	The Genealogist	35
	The Book	36
	Beyond the Life I Lead	37
Rose Donaldson	The Five Gates	39
	Bringing in the Vines	40
	Role Reversal	41
John Evenden	Bad	43
	Lottery	44
	Chemicals	45
Faith Gardener	Peaty and Smoky the Distillery Cats	47
Colven Gibson	Sad	49
Liz Houghton	Dressing Down	51
	Dream Catcher	52
	Supermarket Checkout	53
Mandy Hoy	Whispers	55
Stephen Kingsnorth	Rude Jesus	57
	Honestly	58
	Proscribed - Poetry on Prescription	59

Contents   Page

Author	Title	Page
Jeff Lawrence	Legs	61-62
	Emerging from the Lock down	63
Mark Mardell	Eyes	65-66
Martin Pickard	New Beginnings	69
	08.30 England	70
	Irresistible	71
Stella Pierides	Reflecting	73
	Flying Horse	73
	Alpine Views	73
	Spring Air	73
	Cold Dawn	73
Jim Read	Lost Words	75
	Ode to Spell Checker	75
	Night Writer	75
Tim Roberts	More Than My Doubts	77
	Wild and Hungry	78
	When All My Efforts Come Up Short	79
Alistair Scott	Upon opening My Mother's Typewriter	81
	First Frost	82
	Dreaming Beans	83
John Smith	Ode to Dyskinesia	85
	French Dressing	86-87
Dawson Stafford	Shadow	89
	A New Dawn, A New Day	90
	Winter Coastline	91
Keith Trayling	Horns of Uncertainty	93
	Gardeners Delight	94
	Lost	95
Darrell Troon	Sleep Eludes Me	97
	Winter Awakens	98
	Rope	99
David Urwin	Where Were You When the Deckchairs Were Washed Away?	101
	This and That	102
	A Spot ov bovver wiv vat ole parkinsonz	103
Joe van Koeverden	Focus on a Life with PD	106
	Fred's Not Here Anymore	105
	Medicine of Choice	107
Julie Walker	Cured (I am not)	109-110

Jon Best

I am 55 and a 100% Cornish. My Cornish sense of humour often plays a part in my poetry. I was diagnosed with Parkinson's 17 years ago and my writing has helped me come to terms with some of the changes it brought. I still work full time and regard myself to be a dedicated family man.

Melted Memories

A rarity in my childhood, snow seldom fell in Cornwall.
When it did, fell on the moors, white mischief not seen or heard.
No snowballs or snowman,
No sledging or skiing

So often an avalanche of expectations,
That just melted away under the winter sun.
Nighttime laid a white blanket before dawn,
Wonder revealed by curtains, to 11 years eyes.

Confetti swirled drifting downwards, ghosting the landscape.
A white sheet spread out in all directions.
Rumours of school closure spread by Chinese whispers,
Are made real by radio, verified by accents of authority.

Flurries of jubilant snowballs, ambush the unwary,
Pelting their targets who exercise their right to reply.
Larger balls of snow are rolled and compacted.
As the snowmen's invasion commences,

Footprints in the snow followed my cold feet.
Tramping towards a sloping field on a hill,
My gloved hands, clutching a rectangular metal tea tray,
A makeshift vehicle to skim down the steep meadow.

by Jon Best

Cruel

Elegant heartache
Eyes blinkered by good times
Promises made now shaken
Future imperfect
Tense rules made to be broken
With a ring marital pledge
With a ring discarded
By diagnosis lost its shine
A text within a new context
Of singularity
Carefree but cost too high
Snuffed out match of love
The most beautiful cruel.

by Jon Best

The Grumblebug

Creature has taken up residence
It's in your house and at your expense
Although it slithers just like a slug
It is the grumpy black Grumblebug

The Grumblebug it mutters and moans
With its misery will set the tone
Zaps your energy and saps your will
Charges for services, gives you the bill

Invade your thoughts and enters your mind
Low mood implanted, its tendrils bind
Comfort spending, it divests your wealth
Adds its burden to your mental health

Twisted presence that you cannot unwind
Causes amnesia forget to be kind
Depression and anxiety cause doubt
Self-respect lost, you will live without

Then one day you see your reflection
Grumblebug stares in your direction
Just by instinct you give it a smile
It fades a bit only for a while

You have seen now and you recognise
The Grumblebug it has your own eyes
It is your fears that were brought to life
Allied with worries added to strife

Learning to let go and to forgive
Life is for life and life is to live
Love yourself, embrace the Grumblebug
Surround yourself with the biggest hug

As love grows the black Grumblebug shrinks
Clearing your head then allows you to think
Remember your worth and your value
Happiness returns and hope renews

by Jon Best

Katharina Beyer

Katharina Beyer is a German poet and mother of two young children. She was diagnosed with Early Onset Parkinson's Disease at the age of 34 years. The news came as a shock and writing has helped her to cope. There is not day (or night) that she does not pen something, most of her poetry is in German, but a few years ago started to write poems in English also.

Everywhere

On the ground of facts
on the wings of dreams
in the sea of hope
in the boxes with scrap
in the darkest corner
in the glaring light
under the deepest rubble
behind paper-thin ice
in the smallest hiding places
in the open space
on the biggest posters
in secret notes
it lies hidden
the peaceful path
that despite wild tides
and silent torment
allows you to keep
your balance and grace.

by Katharina Beyer

What I Believe

As in the calming stillness of the meditation
as in trusting awareness of my own beating heart
as in excited fascination of the inhaling breath and the exhaling warmth
as in uttered awe of the complexity of all my body's structure
as in deliberate peace with all my physical limitations
and as in humbled recognition of the unlimited freedom of my mind
as in crazily dedication to all my brave decisions and truthful songs
I dance with my heart wide open on a stable ground.

by Katharina Beyer

The Yorkshire Rose

Through the high grass
of the abandoned site
of frozen dreams
and the stillness of time
where once life moved
the experienced washed down
and the hoped for was drowned
football dreams frenetically celebrated
the loss of comrades soberly swallowed
and the end of each day set on the tap
the place where what seems unbearable in life
weeps politely into the British pale froth
where euphoria and jubilation fall silent to the sound of banter
and rage
and the mundane robs vanity of the exaggerated
a pub on the corner
an English house
where the British wind gently brushes the grass
and though long closed
whispering the stories of the city.

by Katharina Beyer

Tincy Binu

I was diagnosed with Parkinson's disease in September 2019 at the age of 41. I am a nurse working in NHS. I am married and have two boys. Parkinson's diagnosis was an unexpected twist in my life. A nurse who never thought herself being a patient, with a non-curable condition as result I went into a hibernation period till March 2021.
I wrote my first poem on 11th April 2021 on world Parkinson's day. After that wrote few more.

Be a Parkinson

Parkinson's you can't stop me
I am living well at the moment
working with my shaky hands
I believe to live well with Parkinson's
You have to be a PARKINSON

Positivity helps you to go forward
Active nature improves your movements
Resilience helps to face your challenges
Kind to yourself is key to care for own health
Insightful thinking is a power to be purposeful
Nurturing skill will help to support others
Self-confidence is mandatory to carry on
Optimism will help you to achieve dreams
Noble attitude leads you to positive outcome

Parkinson's is not a life sentence
Take time to accept the fact
Be friendly with your new friend
Walk along and adjust yourself
You will find a new life to live

by Tincy Binu

Together Apart

Covid 19 is the pandemic
Whole wide world gone through
And still we are going through
Even in 2021 April....
Covid taught us to stay apart
But being together whilst keeping apart.

A teeny-weeny virus from Wuhan
Which shook the entire world
Local and international restrictions
Lock down, panic buying, job losses ,
Devastated economy, worked from home
Schools closed and we all had to
Stay at home to protect the NHS
To save lives, to be together.

The impact of the pandemic includes
Self-isolation, social distancing
Which made us stay apart with a pain
But it helped all of us to come together.

Loss of loved ones, unable to see dear one
Leads into a mental health crisis for all
We have seen overwhelmed hospitals
With ran out of spaces and equipment
Staff who fought against virus as heroes
Still fighting to regain the backlogs... salute!!

We learned to do virtual events
Staycations, transformation of
Our own gardens to parks
But worries, anxiety and stress
Overruled everyone including children
Whilst we were swimming in the
Darkest days of our entire life (hopefully)
The light appeared at the end of the tunnel
By our brilliant scientists.... vaccine!!
Am I scared to take it, yes, I was ....
But did I take it, YES, I did!!!!
Why??? To protect me, my family & society

We're in this together to support
Sadly, we needed to stay apart
With a hope that we can Unite,
Celebrate together again and again
With our family, friends, and colleagues
Believe everyone, the BETTER DAYS
coming to keep us TOGETHER ....

by Tincy Binu

Alison Blevins

Ali Blevins liked writing poems when she was small, then she grew up and forgot all about it. In 2017 she was diagnosed with Parkinson's disease and shortly after joined Parkinson's Art. That's when Ali discovered she had a lot more stories and poems inside of her head that needed to get out. She is now an active member of 'Poets with Parkinson's' and enjoys writing and sharing all kinds of poetry.

Self Portrait

It starts as a want, a need,
an itch that has to be scratched
and the rest of the world fades away.

Without thinking,
'Am I dressed for this?'
'Should I be doing something else?'
You sweep away the clutter.

Eyes closed you reach in deep for the bones,
tracing their contours with your mind,
drawing them to the surface
so you may lay them out upon the paper.

Millimetre by millimetre,
mark by mark,
adjusting position and form.
Stroking the canvas
until the briefest elements of life appear
and its desire to be nurtured.

Mixing cadmium red and yellow,
Titanium white, a hint of ultramarine blue
you pull flesh from the paint.
Nuances of colour, round peaches, and pinks
plump reds, sunken purples.

Layer upon layer you caress the bones.
until she appears,
emerging from the canvas
eyes watching you,
asking to be made whole.

by Alison Blevins

Some Days

Some days I want like to curl up small like a ball.
I would roll up tight. Coil around my soft insides
And only offer my back, knees, and elbows to the world.
And I would be impenetrable.

Some days I want like to lie out flat on the cool ground.
I would spread myself out until I was so thin -
I would be transparent like the wings of a dragonfly.
You could walk over me without noticing.

Some days I want like to whirl like a hurricane.
I would spin faster than the Waltzer at the fair
I would be a blur of colours sucking up everything in my path
And then I would spit out a rainbow.

Some days I want like to howl and yowl like a wolf at the moon.
I would bellow till my belly bursts and my lungs tear apart
I would wail, shriek and screech like a banshee
And break the sound barrier with my noise.

Some days I want to stretch my limbs until they are like pins.
I would extend my arms until they were so thin, they could pierce skin.
I would be an untouchable, spiky thing,
And I would spear everything in my path.

Some days I want to lie out flat on the cool ground.
I want my belly to touch the earth and feel the worms wriggle
I would dream of warm summer days and cold winter nights
And I would be at peace.

by Alison Blevins

I Lie to You at Least Twice a Day

I lie to you at least twice a day, sometimes I lie more,
I don't know why I lie to you, I'm really not that sure?

I lie about the cake I ate, the last biscuit in the tin,
Why I didn't put the bins out, why I forgot to bring them in.

I lie about who was last, to leave the empty roll,
The toothpaste that has lost its lid and the deodorant I stole.

I lie about the clothes I bought, now hidden in a drawer,
I say I found them in the sale and that they should have cost me more.

But these are inconsequential, because I know that you don't care,
About who ate the last biscuit, or even what I wear.

But then I lie about how tired I am, and say that I slept well,
I'll say the dreams were good ones, when I've really been to hell.

I lie about the pain I'm in, the muscle cramps and aches,
Pretending that it doesn't hurt, the painkillers that I take.

I'll lie about my mood, pretend I'm happy when I'm sad,
Take my frustrations out on paper, so, you won't see me when I'm mad.

I lie to you at least twice a day, to make life easier to bare,
I lie because I love you, I lie because I care.

by Alison Blevins

Valerie Bowden

Valerie is an octogenarian, a retired schoolteacher, with advanced stage of Parkinson's.
She found writing poetry to have a positive effect on dealing with the condition.

Parkinson's Awareness

Those of you who've known me for more than twenty years,
Will have noticed many changes most severe.
We all have aged, that's normal, that all grow old is true
But I've changed more than most, that's very clear.
The reason is that Parkinson's has taken hold of me
And robbed me of a life that was so dear.

I am dependent on my drugs, without them I can't move
With them I can manage to get by.
Reactions are not instant as my muscles don't respond,
I cannot rush no matter how I try.
My face has no expression, it's now a mask like gaze,
There is no more a twinkle in my eye.

I'm often criticised for taking too much drink,
Folk pass me by and keenly they will stare.
They think I am an idiot; they do not realise
That my thoughts remain the same,
I'm still all there. I wish I could speak out loudly,
to raise my voice to tell How Parkinson's does so many lives impair.

I cannot write at all, I cannot even sign my name,
This makes me feel so very, very sad.
I cannot make a phone call or discuss a topic new,
My speech is so unclear, it's very bad.
These things make communication quite a chore,
They are problems that I wish I never had.

Have you ever seen a person trying to cross the road
Looking as if he's had to much to drink
Or a lady struggling at the till to take money from her purse,
Her embarrassment pushing her to the brink?
Maybe you've been forced to stand a long time in the queue
When a woman in front has movement out of sync.

Instead of making her feel much worse if you glare at her and sigh
You could show to her the better side of you.
You could empty out her trolley giving her the chance to pay
The chore's then done more quickly, thanks to you!
As you reflect on the day that's done, you'll wear a smile so wide,
Your action was the best thing you could do.

by Valerie Bowden

Locked Away

I am inside my body looking out, or outside looking in,
trying to hide the woman I've become.
Two persons in one body changing hourly, as life's swing
transforms the lame, mute soul into fleeting perfection.

'On', movements feign normality and I find a place
in the busy, world: though not for long.
'Off' reality is Lord: I am possessed, held by chains,
binding the very heart, controlling every pulse.

Cluttered speech distorts the thoughts that do not reach
my tongue that has become a shroud
Uncooperative lips accompany the smile,
felt, but unseen, falsely portraying me a misery.

I am a prisoner whose cage is one's own body,
forced to dance a dervish or held close, motionless.
Fleetingly, moments of peace tease
as hope leaps into belief that all is well.

No escape is there, no second path to follow.
as locked out, or locked in, I am alone, an isolate,
Looking out or looking in at a body without life,
as future, present, past merge into one

by Valerie Bowden

Jarlath Busby

I was diagnosed with PD in 2017 at the age of 52. I first developed an interest in poetry following my diagnosis, partly to fill the void of being forced to give up my work as a veterinary surgeon. I feel very much a novice at poetry and most of my efforts are unapologetically simple. Humour is my main coping mechanism and I try to incorporate it into my writing. Having grown up in Ireland, I went to Edinburgh Uni and Scotland has been my home ever since. I now live in Fife with my wonderful wife Dawn and Bridie our Boxer.

A Winters Tail

Shrill phone pierces the small hours
Wrenched from my warm pit, duty calls
Heifer calving- making nothing of it
An out the side job

The night is deathly still, not a soul is stirring
All around the suffocating white blanket lies thick
A freezing haar hangs suspended, eerie
Scared to touch this alien landscape
The Lochside road's a Cresta run
Ploughs piled snow drifts above my head
Descend the chute through the amber glowed street
And back into the black void

Steading lights, a siren on the hill
The persistent moth, my trusty Subaru
Bulldozes snow over the bonnet
Must keep moving

Old Sandy waits, knarled and lined
Just watering eyes betray his fear
Like the wide eyes of my patient
Steam rising from her fusing with breath in the cold air
Her thick blood warms my hands
A scarlet pool in the white ground
A glistening calf lands with a slippery wet flop
It's spartan crib of straw and snow

The dark silence heightens the suspense
Only blue-grey instinctive guttural lowing, urging, pleading
Before a blink, a head shake
New life enters this dead of night

by Jarlath Busby

Parkinson's Reveille

As I wake my shaky hand waves and greets me, Hi
Like the class swot catching the teacher's eye
Is it frightened it has slipped my mind?
My affliction's daily incessant grind

I look across and smile at her slumbering eyes
And cuddle her gently as she softly sighs
Is it possible I am the man in her dream?
This Parkinson's wreck with low self esteem

I'd love to sleep as our bodies entwine
But my hand drums a staccato beat on her spine
So, I roll away and every muscle feels stuck
A tear moistens my cheek as I curse my luck

When I lie on my hand, my leg takes up the beat
To some silent tune I'm tapping my feet
No chance for long lies and lazy hugs
My body won't wait on the first dose of its drugs

I would try and ignore it but during the night
My torso's been borrowed for Tyson to fight
Hit like a punchbag and then my legs used
By a marathon runner, all as I snoozed

The worst part of Parkinson's, it's hard to tell
Each day's a smorgasbord of symptoms from hell
No-one likes self-pity, better move this body of mine
Shake a leg! Carpe Diem! Rise and feckin' shine!

by Jarlath Busby

Distant Planets

Love never fully grasped
Planets apart drawn together
Earth and moon

Comforting glow by night
Shaping the day's waves
As the world turns

by Jarlath Busby

Drop of Hope

First snowdrops appear
Optimistic innocence
Starts afresh the year

by Jarlath Busby

Luisa Candela

Luisa was born in 1957 and lives in the northwest of Italy, in a small hill town, located halfway between Turin and the Ligurian Sea. She worked until 2019 as a child psychologist. She has been writing since she was a child and writes from the heart and mind. Following her Parkinson's diagnosis in 2017, she discovered poetry to be an unparalleled creative opportunity.

Dark Inside

Black
Today my day seems black
And I can't see my best
To rest

Night
I'm waiting for the light
And dreaming something fine
To shine

But
If I got so much life
I can't forget the mean
I've seen

So
I want wake up and go
Towards the star I see
For me

by Luisa Candela

Music in the Dawn

I wake up early this morning
Walking fast in the silent street
Everyone is sleeping
The air is quite fresh
I am listening to my breath
And my steps set the pace

Far away a sound
The morning
As dawn is coming
with its soft colours

Sound rising
In the silent city
In the sleeping sand
concert at dawn

by Luisa Candela

Living Anyway

Out of the blue
Not easy to do,
But I felt alone
No one can help me
And with suspicion they look
To my symptoms not to me

Out of the blue
Not easy to do
When my action and my thought
Were hurt by my sickness
And I lost my real hope
To communicate my soul

Out of the blue
My faith goes down,
I try to try,
I hope to hope
I smile to learn
To live anyway
And don't forget
How great is life.

by Luisa Candela

Alice Carroll

Alice has been a member of the Parkinson's community since 2007. Originally from Baton-Rouge U.S.A. but now resides in Virginia. She is known for her creatively funny and quirky poetry and a great storyteller. "Writing poetry does not come naturally to me, but If I bring a smile to any readers, then mission accomplished".

My Parkie Bizarro World of Dreams

Dreams or not
Offer comfort or what?
Foreboding or
Entertaining?
Dare I tell anyone of my dreams,
Lest I'll be placed in a psych ward,
drooling even more.

My Parkie World of Dreams is hard to describe.
Only two types of dreams to ride.
Dream 1. Like a nice episode of "This Is Your Life,"
Who knew my family was so nice?
There is one problem. My dead mother won't leave.
Is she trying to comfort to me?

Dream 2. Like an Alice in Wonderland- animated film, or a fun house at a fair.
A vivid dream with spinning beds, undulating floors, and floating chairs.
Most senses heightened, even smells and tastes.
Except my sense of rhythm remains a disgrace.
As the world spins around, making me dizzy,
I lay flat gripping the bed, almost in a tizzy.

Upon waking, not wanting to part with reality, I run through a checklist at my behest.
- Furniture moved back from whence it came.
- Reconcile there are just the two of us in the house,
- Look for dead relatives lurking about.
- Make sure my legs are in land mode.
Before my grip on the mattress will let go.

by Alice Carroll

Unidentified

Sitting on a park bench, licking my wounded pride
Just viewed a web page of the hood where I grew up
In every photo, I was marked as unidentified.
Even "what's-his-name" was ID'ed in a photo in a pub.
Being shy and mousy, my goal in school was to hide.
Not letting anyone inside.
In that regard, I was a success, I guess.

Breathing deeply to calm myself,
a scrap of paper floated above my lap.
I slammed my hand on the paper so it couldn't budge.
Was this a note from God? I've been known to be a gullible sap.
I'll tell you more and let you be the judge.
Two words, "I Will," were written at the top.
Did the words mean make a list of new year resolutions
That will satisfy my need for retribution.

by Alice Carroll

Downsize

PD finances! What should we do?
We chose option number two,
A senior retirement centre; sounds like a blast.
Our financial guru predicted how long our money would last.

All that money saved for old age will disappear in 15 years.
The senior retirement centre will get our legacy.
Figures don't match our life expectancies
Downsize.

by Alice Carroll

Debbie Dalton

Debbie Dalton is a mother, Grandmother and Great grandmother living in a village in the north of England. Caring for children, with complex needs and needing palliative care. She has written poetry for many moons. Her unwanted guest Parkinson's found her years ago and poetry keeps her grounded and is her escape.

The Genealogist

I walk through the ancients, the ancestors.
My fingertips touch the paper
Whispering their names.

I'm walking softly as a breeze
stirring the ashes and memories
so many stories,
so many tears, so much laughter.

Kinfolk have left their legacies
Some wrapped in puzzles or hidden
I find the strands of webs they have left
begin to weave their tale
For those who are to come.

I do not feel I am intruding
The kinfolk gives me great warmth and welcome
knowing they are still remembered.

by Debbie Dalton

The Book

My favourite time of day is four and five in the morning,
There is a stillness then, that leaves at?
I do not know when
The cats patiently await at window pane
As I sip my coffee
Listening to the gentle patter of what could be rain

My eyes surrendered upon a book
Empty pages, leather bound
A thought, this is the perfect origin
To write a moment I will be captured in the day
Just one line
A smile from who knows who
A thought of someone loved
Penned, valued on the page.
To be found with wonder at a later stage.

by Debbie Dalton

Behind the Life I Lead

Behind The life I lead...
My double life
Make an effort to engage, though I feel lost
In a noisy world.

Make my face smile
Because my face forgets to look interested.

Plan my furniture walk from one room to another
Anticipate where you might freeze.

Get my timing right to stand up
It's going to hurt and be awkward
Remember to make it look easy.

And then there is the dreaded question asked
How are you?
I am fine, an automated reply.

Maybe tomorrow will be a better day
In my double life.

by Debbie Dalton

Rose Donaldson

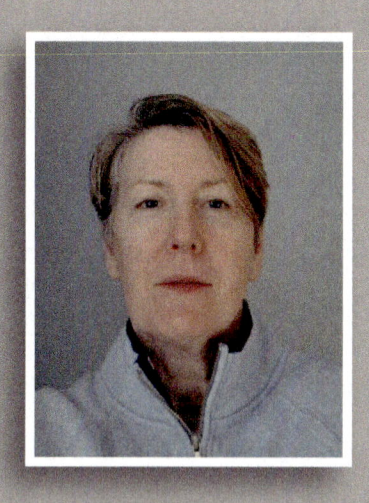

My name is Rose, and I am the mother of 3 boys living in Scotland for the last 4 years. Previously living just outside London for nearly 30 years. I was diagnosed with PD in 2016 which coincided with me leaving my job as long-haul cabin crew after 25 years.

Five Gates

Gravel crackling under foot
Grass creeping over untended verges
Rotting fences rendered useless by the wind and rain
The bluetit, blackbird, crow and the rook
Disturbed by the crunchy stomp approaching
They take flight swiftly finding refuge
On the wafer-thin branches of the fir trees
Sheep graze idly on the sloping rocky hills
Only glancing up lazily to show derision
Passing through one of the five rusty gates brings new sights
Either Aberdeen, Ayrshire, Shetland and Highland coos
Munch greedily on the wild and plentiful grasses
Before loping down the hillside to be milked
The creaking of the decades old gate doesn't deter them from their mission
The vista on a clear day from the old Victorian pipeline
Opens up to the glistening loch in the distance framed by the Munros
The view ends abruptly when the mighty oak blocks the passage through the fifth gate
Completing this feast for not just the eyes but the mind, body, and soul.

by Rose Donaldson

Bringing in the Vines

The early morning haze beckons the throng from slumber
The blue hued vines await and loll in readiness to drop
Gravel crunches under the feet of those who will share the toil
Baskets lined up along the rows while gloves pulled on and sharp props at the ready.

Vine virgins hesitate with nervous glances as experience cuts through
Pulling back the branches reveals the juice laden triangle of berries
Snip, drop, catch and throw a system learnt and a rhythm continued
As brows are mopped in the rising sun drinks are proffered.

Baskets are filled, renewed and topped up to be taken across fields
The vines are now empty, been checked by the expert who rebuffs those sun singed grapes
As the final baskets are loaded, chatter , laughter and relief welcomes the rain
Drops cool and soothe the redness and heat on the sun parched necks.

Their labour much appreciated needs celebrated and thanked
The food and drink spread like a feast for the masses
No morsel left untouched; gratitude understood as the table empties
Promises given for favours, help and sustenance returned.

by Rose Donaldson

Role Reversal

I will always wonder how I got here
When I was the one who followed you
I jumped when you deigned to look at me
I ran after you when you turned away.
You walked around with an ego so high
I gazed in awe that you had such sway.

I crossed the water to get out of your glare
I grew in stature, allure and became
A woman of substance with no ties
But experience taught me to hold a little back
Leave the room with longing eyes gazing
Maybe tilt your head slightly to see the strength crack.

Thirty years later you honestly thought
I'd be falling at your knees when you appeared suddenly.
My God you had changed, it was like role reversal
I had too, though battered and bruised
I knew who I was, who I am and who matters
Your plan to seduce me left me bemused.

These days I take things a little bit slower
Your life seems to have all but stopped
You're still waiting to collect on a promise
Made when we both had hopes and fears unknown
The difference being I reached for the stars with the love of my only
Looking down, left too late you're now on your own.

by Rose Donaldson

John Evenden

I used to be John Evenden, happy with my life at peace, I've had a few knocks, who hasn't? I'd carved myself a niche. But Parkinson's struck, and took me away, and left an imposter who's tormented every day.

Bad

How bad does it get, this Parkinson's disease?
I would like to know; can you tell me please?
But who to ask, how much to know?
Look to the future, or go with the flow?

I see people on telly, their symptoms look severe,
I don't want to be like them, nowhere near.
I want to be normal, get my old life back,
Ditch this illness, get my life back on track.

It is what it is, I gotta live with this s**t
Feeling shaky, slow, and stiff, my escape is a hit.
Synthetic dopamine, that's what I feel,
It works wonders for me, the results are real.

As I've said before, a hit doesn't last long,
It only gives a glimpse, so you have to stay strong.
It was discovered a while ago, about for 50 years
But what since then? I have my fears.

Is this the answer, is this all they've got?
I rather hope it isn't, I rather hope not.
I live in hope, that they'll find a cure,
Then I can live my life, a good one for sure,

by John Evenden

Lottery

Roll up, roll up, everyone's a winner,
Let's determine your fate, whether a saint or a sinner.
Pour the balls in a bucket and select your fate.
What will it be? One you'll like or one you'll hate?

You've been good to others, so deserve a break,
So, select a ball, let's see the man you'll make.
You dig deep, and think, "this is my time",
You pull out green, number 49.

The lady in charge checks her sheet,
Then appears awkward, and stares at her feet.
I'm afraid you've just won a degenerative disease,
Oh no, not me God, not me God, please.

But this is your fate, you have to accept,
There's no going back, no one's exempt.
You selected Parkinson's, and that's your lot,
Not a rich man you, good fortune you have not.

Maybe its punishment for past lives they can't forgive,
Or maybe it's the price, for rewards in lives yet to live.
Or maybe it just proves life's a lottery,
You have no control, what will be, will be.

by John Evenden

Chemicals

This collection of chemicals, is not very good,
Go back and get a remix? Not sure I would.
Too much of one thing, not enough of another,
It's just my inheritance from my father and mother.

It's no one's fault, it's the family tree,
But why end up contaminating me?
It's who you are, it's what makes you, you,
You can't pick and choose, it's not possible to do.

Cos if you did, you'd be someone else,
And who's to know the state of their health.
So, accept it, get on with your life and deal with it,
Play the cards you're dealt, do not quit!

by John Evenden

Faith Gardner

I live in the West of Scotland and am now retired but I love words and perhaps due to a positive side effect of my PD medication find myself to be a poet. I wrote the poem after meeting Peatey on a visit to the Kilchoman Distillery on Islay last year and never forgetting about Old Possum. One day there may be more.

The Distillery Cats

Peaty and Smokey are the Distillery cats.
Kilchoman is where they are HOME.

They greet you and inspect you and check you up and down,
When you walk through the archway of Rockside Farm.

At Rockside Farm whisky is made, barley is grown, and lambs are born.
And at this place two wild kittens are found.
They hiss and squeal and scratch and fight.
But those two brothers have made it their site.

Peaty and Smokey became the Distillery cats.
Kilchoman is where they are HOME.

They patrol the lambing sheds, and all the staff.
They might drink some milk that is mostly for the lambs,
But really the boys enjoy the atmosphere, as the barley moves along,
As the acrosphere grows and the peat is smoked,
As the grist is formed and the Mash Tun fills.

Peaty and Smokey are the Distillery cats.
And Kilchoman is where they are HOME.

At Rockside farm Kilchoman whisky is created.
The bottles gleam and shine as they roll off the production line.
Labelled and dated and moved onwards to be mated
With a careful eager owner whose wish to own a
Kilchoman amber liquid is thus sated.

Peaty and Smokey are the Distillery cats.
They greet you and inspect you and check you up and down
Whilst you too select your favourite of the range.
Happy with your choice you raise a dram in praise

Of Peaty and Smokey, the Distillery cats.
And Kilchoman where they are HOME.

by Faith Gardner

Colven Gibson

My name is Colven Gibson, also known as Geordie Parr, as you might have guessed I am from Newcastle upon Tyne. I was pushed onto the Parkinson's rollercoaster in the summer of 2015, but I am still working full time. I had been contributing to the Poetry section of Parkinson's UK, this introduced me to Radio Parkies, where my work was broadcast to the World. In turn, the radio work led me to the Parkinsons Art website.

Sadness

An open book, infectious smile
A rollercoaster, mile after mile
Hidden talents, lurked within
So much promise, that did not begin

For many years we failed to meet
Not by design, life is that way
Then the Fates declared we should greet
For both of us, a happy day

I saw so many things in you
That were also inside me
And I doubt not that my memories few
For the rest of my days will stay complete

So please don't fill my grave with tears
Let happiness be your souvenirs
Let my forebears hear me come
Let me arrive in raucous style

Or remember me in a favourite song
Fast or slow, none are wrong
The melodies those songs will bring
Will become mine, for I will also sing

by Colven Gibson

Liz Houghton

I was diagnosed with Parkinson's in 2014. Having always written the occasional poem, production increased during the pandemic: leading to the publication of my first book. Two subsequent books followed and I now tour around Bedfordshire giving recitals to raise money for Parkinson's Table Tennis, my favourite pastime.

Dressing Down

The biggest challenge of the day
Is getting dressed - once child's play.
I don't know which garment's worse
If you ask me each one is cursed.

Pants are where the nightmare starts
And my sanity soon departs
Feeble hands clutch tight elastic
A miracle now would be fantastic!

Nothing gets me more depressed
Than wrestling with my wretched vest
And when I finally get it on
I can feel I've got it wrong

The whole thing now is front to back
And I'm at great risk of heart attack!
The entire procedure takes an age
And soon I start to rant and rage

I simply want to tuck it in!
But it seems I cannot win
My despair is quite profound
I don't have time to mess around.

Socks and shoes, need I say more?
You and I both know the score.
I try to bend down to my feet
But sense the onset of defeat.

The time has come to make a stand -
I hope that you will understand.
I don't intend to cause a sensation...
But I've joined the Naturist Foundation!

And as everybody knows -
Members there dispense with clothes.
Nudity is not a sin
I know that I will fit right in.

by Liz Houghton

Dreamcatcher

The rush of thoughts I have each day
Spills out in such a random way.
I often feel I'm in a trance
Watching ideas swirl and dance.

My thoughts and feelings mesmerise
They bob and weave before my eyes.
I know if I don't write them down
They'll disappear and go to ground.

I find I have to be prepared
Now my memory's so impaired.
That's why I scribble lots in books
Making notes that act like hooks.

I list the things that I must do
To get me through each day anew.
And then, of course, there are my rhymes -
Oddball ideas and half baked lines.

These must be caught with pen and ink
Or they'll be gone, quick as a wink.
But how am I to read my scrawl
Now that my writing's very small?

Strange shapes that look like hieroglyphs
Gather in great heaps and drifts.
They stretch themselves across the page
Deciphering them takes an age.

This is how I write my verse
My methods can be quite perverse.
Gradually I'm getting worse
Time for my medication nurse!

by Liz Houghton

Supermarket Checkout

I get to the checkout and reach for my purse
I can't find it of course and silently curse.
How hard can it be to pay up and go?
Why am I now so impossibly slow?

Aware that people behind me are starting to queue
I upend my bag and start to hunt through.
There are too many pockets, too many folds
My hesitant fingers won't do what they're told.

Lots of compartments that serve to confuse
This is all part of the shopping day blues.
At last I am done and can't wait to get out
But I hear a loud noise and somebody shouts.

It seems I've set off the blasted alarm!
But it wasn't me, I've done them no harm.
I have to wait while my shopping is viewed
Personally I think it's terribly rude.

And as it turns out it's their fault, not mine
They've left the tag on a bottle of wine.
And now I blush red as if I'm accused
Of drinking too much and they're all amused.

The way that I trip and stumble and sway
They obviously think I indulge every day.
I think for a mo should I try to explain?
But decide in the end that there's nothing to gain.

And so I lurch home, not sure what to think
But one thing's for sure - Parkinson's stinks!

by Liz Houghton

Mandy Hoy

I was born in November 1963 and work in social care in the city of Nottingham. I was diagnosed with Parkinson's in 2013 at the age 46 and a sudden compulsion to be creative drove me to start painting. Then the verses started to come into my head, and I found painting and writing poems controlled the demons.

Whispered

The devil whispered in my ear
Just watch while I break you
I turned around and began to laugh
That's one thing you'll never do

Cos wo betide,
with my army by my side
I will put up one hell of a fight

And it's very rare
That I ever scare
Especially when I know I'm right

Bring it on
I'm prepared and strong
I'll do whatever it takes

I'm ready now
I'll show you how
You'll see how a hero's made

So come and dance
Take a chance
Devil if you dare

But think on this
Watch whatever you dish
Cos one day I might end up down there.

by Mandy Hoy

Stephen Kingsnorth

I retired to Wales, from ministry in the Methodist Church due to Parkinson's Disease and had pieces curated and published by on-line poetry sites, printed journals, and anthologies. I have been nominated for the Pushcart Prize and Best of the Net.

Rude Jesus

Blunt, rude and offensive,
so not the simply winsome man
I had presumed as a teen.

On course, I do not know
how much he said
or earliest church gospellers
thought he said, or told he said,
or wanted him to have said.
or thought the spirit tell he said.

But curt frequency suggests
there is verisimilitude;
whited sepulchres, too good a phrase
describing worst religion's haze,
the smog hypocrisy that dims the light
and barriers peace, hope and love.

Mat man, I read, was told to walk
but likely to his rest resumed,
unflattered that this one dare speak
to him that way, who was so old.
The foreign woman, requesting whole,
is told to wait, wag puppy tail;
although she gives as good as get
and so, unlocks said miracle.

Blind man is sent through the crowds
dripping mud and spit from brows;
leader's daughter mourned for cash
all sent packing, given push.
Even parents dealt poor hand
when outside, waiting in the sand.

Disciples get the harsher tongue,
always told they'd had more time,
so really should have more than clue
who he is and what to do;
in Galilean carnival
thus, this man is critical.
Who is this Jesus, rood man?

by Stephen Kingsnorth

Honestly

A closet life until my wife,
the cloister monk, set single sex,
11+ Grammar, Boys of course,
until Advanced, then year off course.
Gap YM, see a hostel year -
females banned beyond the stair -
thence to Cambridge, male college days.
There were no *femmes, fatale* or not,
except my sisters - didn't count.
No such peerless amongst my peers,
nor lip service when unscene seen.
Free love sixties, or flower power
were more of Nam, house rising sun.
I wasn't there, that Woodstock gen -
for I was Shakespeare, Kubla Khan,
and captivated Gerard Man.
What girl wants Wordsworth, Shelley, Keats,
which boy befriends the poet swot?
So hear, this nil return is mine,
for cannot write of what don't know.
You think it strange, naïvety?
I count it blessing, no disguise.
So take me, others, as we are,
Judaeo-Christian, sheltered lives,
primed by poets, and so thought strange,
but pride in age, creatively.
Fiction is not my métier;
so please forgive my honesty.
Another failure to conform;
I only take me as I am.

by Stephen Kingsnorth

Proscribed - Poetry on Prescription

My classes, Dance with Parkinson's
have proved more balanced than I thought,
though, fraught, I first appliqué sought,
but with bent knees, a plié taught.
In flexing joints, I joined the corps -
as you surmise, like one, next day -
on Zoom, screened from field summer play,
as others basked, sunscreen as faced.
I'm at the bar - as others are -
me drinking in new moves afoot,
and arabesque, beer belly hang.
I asked it of the PD Nurse -
how no one treating of the curse
had ever measured prancing worth?
She charged she'd never witnessed it,
said culture was the better source
of finance for such upper crust.
My next enquiry was to be
about prescribing poetry,
but then I realised that verse
was filed, like ballet, not my class.

by Stephen Kingsnorth

Jeff Lawrence

I'm Jeff I've had Parkinson's for 10 years, and my poetry is inspired largely by my Parkinson's experience. Some are serious and others funny. I hope they give you a laugh. Having not written a poem in my life before my diagnosis no one was more surprised that me to find this creative skill. I have now written over 40 poems. I sometime write under the pseudonym of shaky spear!

Legs

Legs are really wonderful
They carry us around
They stop us all from falling
Keeping both feet on the ground.

But what if they stop listening
Just like a naughty child
Refusing all requests
And simply running wild.

Parkinson's can do that
It can takes away control
But it does it very sneakily
Bang you're in a hole.

It can strike you without warning
Leave you struggling to stand
Make you feel rather embarrassed
Cos that's not what you'd planned.

In the street it may just freeze you
Super glue you to the spot
Come on legs behave yourself
Let's just give it one more shot.

In the pub some people stare
As your walking with a slew
You can hear them gently whispering
Bet he's just had a few.

Even going for a wee
Such a simple task
Becomes a major undertaking
God I wish I had a mask.

Come on legs don't mess about
I need you to be free
This takes on more urgency
When you need a pee!

So you give your legs encouragement
Come on you two behave
It's really rather simple
I don't want to be your slave.

The "grand old duke of York"
Now I'm singing to my legs
In the pub the whispering continues
"God that man he's just the dregs".

But my Parky pals will know
What it's like when legs won't budge
And all I ask of others
Is don't be so quick to judge.

Stop and ask if we're ok
Not just pass us in the street
And just be really, really grateful
That you've got two working feet.

Love and value your legs
Cos it's true you only miss things when their gone.

by Jeff Lawrence

Emerging from Lockdown

Happy new year sounds a bit optimistic
As we rush to study the latest statics
Omicron is surging of that there's no doubt
Whilst restrictions and fear have stopped us going out.

We've been here before in this strangest of years.
Some have felt stressed while others shed tears.
Some lost their jobs and with it their pride
As the virus mutates leaving nowhere to hide

.For others their business has gone to the wall
Some employed many whilst others were small.
Hospitality and travel were particularly hard hit
Many staff found they had no choice but to quit.

But enough of the past we know it's been tough
But if your still standing for now that's enough.
Our sense of what matters has come to the fore.
Our family our friends who we've missed more and more.

So take time to reflect on this strangest of years.
And the lessons it taught us as it challenged our fears.
The tunnel was long but there's a light at the end
Let's not forget those on whom we depend.

The doctors, the nurses, the teachers, our police
As they try to struggle to heal us, or keep the peace
Also spare a thought for our retail assistants
Whose roles make it difficult to socially distance

So many to thank the list is so long
If I got my way they would all get a "gong"
With the booster success we have something to cheer
As our chance of defeating this virus draw near.

As our thought turn to things we enjoyed for so long
Let's learn the lessons from when things all went wrong
As we emerge from the tunnel back into the light
That "Happy New Year" might just be in sight.

by Jeff Lawrence

Mark Mardell

Mark Mardell is one of six presenters of the 'Movers and Shakers' podcast, about living with Parkinson's. Before he retired, he had been at the forefront of reporting and analysing major world events on TV and radio for 25 years, for the BBC. He lives in Surrey with his wife Jo. They have three grown-up children who are their pride and joy. He is slowly shedding his lifelong obsession with world politics and replacing it with an equally obsessive interest in new music, writing odd poems and making wonky pottery.

Eyes

Eyes like drenched violets
Highs like trenched violence
thighs like wanton pirates
To rise in flounce euphoric and twirl,
a boyish bounce then a gamine whirl
everything becomes this knighting girl
enrapturing, capturing
the saucy unslaked sad eyes
of benched pilots and celibates
celebrants all, warming their icy hands
on the glow of her scarlet starlight

II
He sighs as honeyed starlets' pirouettes
wrench worlds away in a mooncalf daydream
What shall we call it?
A dream in a ruined castle
An old man's folly
This performative pantomime of lust
Untimely, ungainly, unmanly
Or holy water flung against rust
and fast approaching dust
"a limerence" Old Tweedy pronounces
Huffing stale shag,
Glasses sliding down his long nose
Next door huffs and tuts

In a faded, fated dressing gown
'plum' according to the brochure
"Disgusting, that's what I call it
What's he thinking, at his age"
For we must and will have a chorus,
Not high kicking, but all low blows and stamped toes
She and her kith guard the gates of propriety
Holding aloft in triumph
flint flakes of insanity
(sparkling struck cock lathered insanitary)

They burn with profound banality,
Flaming with equal delight: Mr Toad
For multiple breaches of the highway code
Gypsy child's hankering for an open road,
A painted peoples' delight in ink and woad
And the horned hierophants of unfashionable gods
Struggling to absorb the latest restrictions on oysters, blood
sacrifice, occasional vice and unrestricted joy
And he, he polices their minds with equal ardour
Using science as a pretext, Using subtext as a scalpel
slicing and dicing, calibrating creation
To divide and fool, each cut creating a new rule
To parse smoke and parcel souls into little pots
Locking in a box the star lit silver fox.

by Mark Mardell

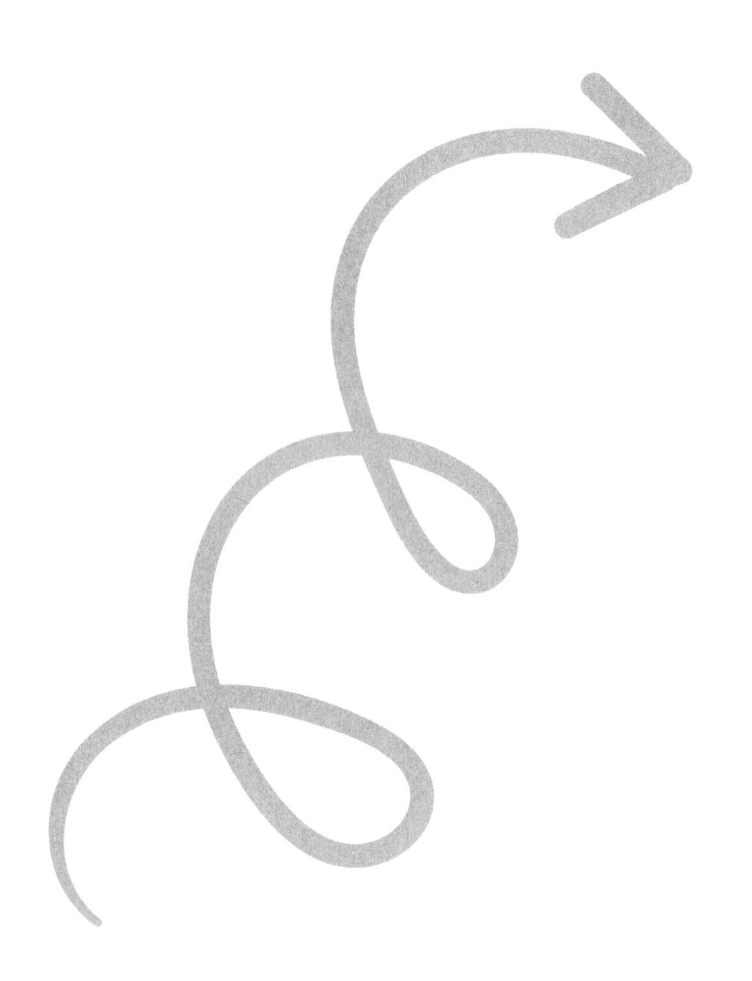

Martin Pickard

Martin Pickard describes himself as a Shaken Word poet from Bedfordshire in the UK and is one of the co-founders of Poets with Parkinson's. He was formally diagnosed in 2020 after several years of uncertainty during which he started to write poetry both for therapy and to satisfy a new creative urge. He has hosted online poetry events since 2021 and enjoys performing his work live at local open mic nights.

New Beginnings

"Before people can begin something new, they have to end what used to be and unlearn the old way". William Bridges

In the beginning, life is good.
One foot follows another
with purpose.

But the ending is familiar and
comfort and apathy distract me
from the perpetual need for change.

In the lawless land
between ending and beginning there lies
a pandemonium of possibilities.

Shall I begin?

by Martin Pickard

08.30 England

Icy wind and incinerator steam drifts aimlessly across the valley

Some unspoken order sends the sheep marching single file to a warmer pasture

Two boys, caps back, with matching Minecraft packs, trail reluctantly behind a stressed mother, desperate to make the school on time

Other mothers pass her, already heading home, freed of their charges they chatter like schoolgirls planning a dance

Echoes of playground laughter run around the nearby churchyard, where blowsy daffodils droop in silent tribute and fresh-faced snowdrops eagerly await the day

A lonely glove waits hopefully on a handy branch and discarded poo bags loiter by the community centre, blackbirds take up position on the deserted cricket pitch

On such a day great poets learn to read; engineers begin to dream and lifetime lovers hold hands for the first time.

The bell rings

by Martin Pickard

Irresistible

Cursing his stupidity, the unwary thief
writhes naked on the silken sheet,
trap-woven from cords of steel,
sticky as the spilled syrup on the kitchen floor
that had been so very tempting
Each twist and turn against the ties
send twitching tremors of terror
down the wire and into the dark
alerting her motionless, malevolent magnificence

She's been waiting for days, weeks.
Patient in her monstrous beauty
No food or drink since her last late lover
Her dark and dead-pool eyes see little now
but oh, how she feels...
Unlike her prey she is not heartless
Irresistible venom whets her captivating smile
and with stunning speed, she makes her move
leaving him drained and empty
Desiccated by the beautiful cruel.

by Martin Pickard

Stella Pierides

Stella Pierides's books include "Of This World" (2017) and "In the Garden of Absence" (2012), both HSA Merit Book Award recipients. Her article "Parkinson's Toolbox: The Case for Haiku" appeared in Juxtapositions: A Journal of Research and Scholarship in Haiku, issue 8, 2022. Stella serves on the Board of Directors of The Haiku Foundation (THF) and manages the THF's Haiku for Parkinson's feature.

Reflecting

reflecting
on the sky's glorious depths...
sweet chicory

Flying horse

flying horse
the merry-go-round
of childhood

Alpine views

Alpine views ...
filling the heart
with space

Spring Air

the spring air
studded with blooms...
morning grace

Cold Dawn

cold dawn...
trees dressed
in moonlight

by Stella Pierides

Jim Read

Writing and editing were an important part of my working life. In 2013, aged 62 I was diagnosed with Parkinson's. I found myself, for the first time, writing monologues, plays and the occasional poem. From this grew a performance piece, Swimming in Air, inspired by my joyful experience of a dance for Parkinson's class. I like the mix of inspiration, craft and graft which goes into writing a poem and learning to live with imperfection.

Lost Words

Words emerge
Hinting at the possibility of a poem
Most disappear before I catch them
Leaving a glimpse of an idea
And a touch of despair.

It's a blessing and a curse
The urge to play with words
And memory loss.

by Jim Read

Ode to Spell Check

By a bad speller and worse typer.
Random clusters of vowels and consonants
Turn into words
My spelling checked and corrected
Without criticism.

by Jim Read

Night writer

Scary dreamer
Restless mover
Busy brainer

Sheep counter
Wider awaker
Bed abandoner

Pen and paper
Then remember
Can't decipher

Laptop opener
Blank screen starer
Gotta start somewhere

Free writer
Self-inspirer
Rhyme hunter
Dawn yawner
Sleep succumberer
Slumberer.

by Jim Read

Tim Roberts

Tim Roberts was diagnosed with Parkinson's disease 4 years ago when he was aged 50. A police officer in Britain for many years he now lives with his wife in New Zealand and has three wonderful daughters and one special granddaughter. Tim enjoys nature, the peculiar quality of the sunlight in Aotearoa, the native birds, the wild beaches and the older woodlands and loves taking his dog for walks whenever he can.

More Than My Doubts

Face to face...I see you and through you I see me. I am more than my doubts bigger than my fears and when all my efforts come up short...

When all my efforts come up short
and pleading and howling
my hopes are reduced to naught
I am caught in the dark
lost beaten stripped naked
with every nerve wracked and fraught
then I go to the forest and sit in the rain
letting Life wash through me
and purify me again
and drop by drop by drop
I become a living prayer
and I flow back into this world
trusting
and touching
and caring
and knowing
that all my efforts will come up short
but doing it anyway again.

by Tim Roberts

Wild and Hungry

When I am swamped or overwhelmed I go to a wild beach. The wilder the weather the sooner the beach tames my demons and restores equilibrium...well, equilibrium for me.

vast sky
wlld beach -
one word would be too much

We usually have several kilometres of sand to ourselves - that's me and Albs, an old, deaf dog who doubles as my spiritual director. We were there today, in bright autumn sun. Oyster catchers ignored us as Albs led us off the beach into the dunes behind it. The wind changed direction and became a strong southerly blowing a freeze up from Antarctica and, as always, there is always one cricket still singing the sweetest summer song into the folds of a southerlie. We offered a dune prayer...may we too sing in the wind revelling in life like the crazy crickets...and we pushed on....

next...a hatful of dragons.

by Tim Roberts

When All My Efforts Come Up Short

When all my efforts come up short
and pleading and howling
my hopes are naught
I am caught in the dark
lost, naked, every nerve fraught
then I go and sit in the rain
letting Life wash through me again
and drop
by drop
by drop
I become a living prayer
and I flow back into this world
trusting
and touching
and caring
and knowing
that all my efforts will come up short
and doing it anyway

by Tim Roberts

Alistair Scott

After graduating in agricultural science in the 1960s, I moved from the UK to Africa where he spent 20 years teaching and working for environmental conservation organisations. During that time, I took up writing, winning awards in the BBC Wildlife Awards for Nature Writing. I then went to work for the World Wide Fund for Nature (WWF) at their headquarters in Switzerland and subsequently retired there, to play the clarinet and write poetry.

Upon Opening My Mother's Typewriter

Unclip the silver clasp. Lift off the case.
A tang of oil and ink wafts up from row
on row of keys that stare me in the face,
blank as the eyes of fish. What do they know
about my mother's life? The ribbon, black and red,
is tattered like the flags that flew
above the camps and barracks of the land she fled.
Her father's land. Except her father was a Jew.

What did she write to rip the ribbon so?
What terrors of a refugee did she confide?
Like soil that soaks up blood, the keys will know.
Like blooded soil they hold those secrets tied.

Feed in a sheet of paper, blank and white.
What words are there that I can write?

by Alistair Scott

First Frost

Last night an anticyclone
sidled off the sea and squatted
over Europe,
made the sky arch
clear and brittle.

Through hours of darkness
gangs of starry gods
sucked up the dregs
of summer warmth
and scattered silver winter-seed
across the fields, on clod and blade,
until a sluggish sun arose
to claim the day.
Now in the early morning light
a wasp clings to the wall
outside my kitchen window
feelers flattened to its head,
wings folded low.

Caught by the gods
it bowed before their bitter breath
to wait for death.
But death was slow,
too slow last night and now
the sun swings lowly round.

The wasp's wings shiver in the growing warmth.
It shakes its head from side to side
as if it can't believe it lives,
preens feelers, flexes joints, then

by Alistair Scott

Dreaming Beans

There I was, standing in the supermarket
gazing at the shelf of baked beans,
their cans in ranks like soldiers,
each label a bright biography,

When a cart trundled past, echoing
a thousand buying tales it had heard,
its wheels wobbling out another shopping story
down aisles of mundane miracles.

Around me stretched a maze of shelves
like chapters in a novel of choices,
a narrative of flavours ready to unfold
in the kitchens of the ordinary.

I picked up a bean can,
metal cool against my palm,
and wondered about the beans within,
trapped in their tiny, tiny universe.

Do they dream of the fields
where sun once kissed their tender pods?
Or are they resigned to their fate
as captives in a world of tomato sauce?

The checkout lanes beckoned,
a trundle of conveyor belts,
on which my beans are swept towards freedom
like refugees seeking the safety of a new life.

Then I left, carrying my bag of stories.
The automatic doors sighed shut behind me and
I loaded my groceries into the back of the car.
The world resumed its mundane plod.

As I drove off, I saw, "Save! Budget! Bargain!"
in the rear-view mirror, blazoned over
a cathedral of commerce, where miracles unfold,
and baked beans dream.

by Alistair Scott

John Smith

Diagnosed in 2015 I live in Northeast London. I used to write poetry as a teenager and returned to writing after diagnosis when symptoms started to get more noticeable. Encouraged by family I like to reflect the humour in my situation and life in general. I also enjoy drawing which seems to calm my tremor. Long may it last!

Ode to Dyskinesia

There's nothing quite like dyskinesia It's like a movement amnesia.
The waving of head, the twitching of arms It's really not one of my elegant charms
The brain is a very wonderful thing. Mine is selective in what it can bring,
It just needs enhancing to stop all this dancing.
The dopamine levels all vary and then the movements quite scary.
I shimmy and shake. But just by mistake.
It makes me quite shy, and then when I try
To talk in the group, I'm out of the loop
My volumes too low and I wanted to show
I was part of the chat, but no one hears that
My speech is now fading, I need it upgrading
The process is slow, and I want you to know
I'm as sharp as I was and it's only because
There's a gap before speech when the brains out of reach
Its like there's a filter when my thoughts out of kilter
By the time It's selected the words are rejected
The topic has changed my response would seem strange
It's slow and it's hard to play the Parkinson's card
It's not for faint hearted your brain has departed
From normal responses and your only conscious
That it's not the same which is quite a shame
But friends are the key they get used to me
I'm happy enough even though it is tough

by John Smith

French Dressing

It's out of my range to do a quick change
In moments of passion, it's becoming the fashion
To remain fully dressed haven't you guessed
I made up that line to make me feel fine
When it's time for a shower I need a full hour
The soap is alive it's doing the jive.
With a dopamine pill it may become still
The shampoo is gel it's so hard to tell
I have to confess I needed much less
There's masses of foam will it muck up the chrome?
Two rinses or more to get out the door
At last, I am done it's not been much fun

When did my clothes become sticky and putting them on was more tricky,
Are my arms just too long or my fingers not strong.
For buttons and zips have you any tips?
They fold and refuse whatever I use,
To fit through the gap, they now need a map.
And zips with their teeth are not a relief,
They need careful adjusting it's like they were rusting.
I need Velcro and poppers please tell the shoppers.
No button-down shirts. Could I ever wear skirts?
My pants aren't that easy it's making me queasy,
Two legs down one side "I'm falling." I cried.
"They've a mind of their own" I'm starting to moan.

Each separate sock I have to unlock.
Nobody knows I can't reach my toes.
It's the end of my feet that try to compete,
They get hooked in each garment, that's not their department
My least favourite task is having to ask.
"Can you help me get dressed" I think I'm depressed

Attending the Gents puts me in suspense,
There's looks of surprise as I play with my flies.
It's too difficult there, no wonder they stare.
The sleeves in my jackets are turning to packets,
Where's the hole at the end it sends me round the bend
Would it be rude to just sit in the nude?

I'll get dressed tomorrow and maybe I'll borrow.
A cape or a cloak but that's just a joke.
I'll struggle and try, there's no need to cry,
I'll dress and I'll look like the men in the book.
And no one will know it's the Parkinson's show
If it fits like a glove, then heavens above
I'm now getting obsessed with trying to get dressed
While trying to shave my hands won't behave
Would it be weird to just grow a beard
I'm starting to sweat but I'm not ready yet
One thing that's new I'm sharing with you.
My watch straps elastic it fits me, fantastic!

by John Smith

Dawson Stafford

Born 1965 Birmingham U.K. William Dawson Stafford the son of Irish parents grew up in Belfast during 'The Troubles'. It was here that he met his fiercest critic, his wife Jeanette and go on have two sons. After being diagnosed with Parkinson's in 2012 he discovered that writing poetry was a way of expressing himself whilst creating awareness surrounding the condition.

Shadow

I'm battling a daily shadow
a shadow that can't be seen
Which lurks round every corner
and hides behind the scenes

It waits until your guard is down
then springs a stealth attack
From the outside things are Rosey
but inside your head they're black

Once it gets a hold of you
it's difficult to control
Its persistent, unrelenting
feeding off your very soul

Weapons cannot kill it
but chemicals can contain
this shadow frequently penetrating
the dark recesses of your brain

It retreats from the bombardment
and eventually goes to ground
and returns to the darkness
without making a sound

I've made it through another day
against a shadow I abhor
I have won this latest battle
but am I losing the war?

by Dawson Stafford

Winter Coastline

A watery sun floats on the horizon, tries to squeeze between the clouds
but the grey, menacing stratus, want to keep it down
the swell makes massive breakers, the seas total power unleashed
tossing sea debris from the depths below, high up on the beach

the deafening sound of waves, as they slam against the shore
then hiss like a thousand serpents as they retreat to the sea once more
I tighten my coat around my throat, to shelter from the wind
as the sea spray comes in sideways, to drench us to the skin

a forest of kelp dislodged and washed up on the beach.
a shingle of shells, rocks, and molluscs crunch beneath our feet
the sweet smell of seaweed, dominates the air
while sand flies jump from stem to stem and flit from here to there

pebbles of all colours, shapes, and sizes, eroded over time
lie huddled in little cairns covered in a salty brine
the barking of a dog travels intermittently on the wind
as he runs around playing fetch with his owner on the sand

the drone of a ship's foghorn, echoes through the gloom.
as the glow from the lighthouse on the headland, warns sailors of certain doom.
the foam from the breakers spews over the sea wall
looking like a white, drifting, carpet of snow fall

cormorants cry and swoop above the waves as fish get tossed beneath
diving in a feeding frenzy, Mother Nature's bonus treat
ships cling to the horizon, dancing in harmony with sea
as they limp their way into port to unload their precious bounty

stranded fish in rock pools, left behind upon the shore
seek refuge neath rocks and stones until the tide returns once more

by Dawson Stafford

A New Dawn, a New Day

As darkness fades and bows its head toward the rising sun
shards of light pierce timid clouds, reflect the dew of early morn
a mist clings to the undergrowth in a ghost like vail
as cold air battles warm, it's efforts all in vain

the warming light brings earth to life and the chorus of dawn
you wake to sounds of singing birds, another days begun
the red sky glows intensely from pinks through to maroon
illuminating vapour trails like rockets to the moon

the crystal stream goes gushing by, refracting the sunlight
all the colours of the rainbow in a symphony of light
you shield your eyes from sunlight as you look towards the sky
a Red Kite circles high above watching rodents scuttle by

butterflies dance in silence as they flit among the flowers
in a kaleidoscope of colour, they have but a few hours
blades of grass sway to and fro, like emerald ribbons in the breeze
the screaming of a peacock ricochets through swaying trees

a bird digs for breakfast in the moisture of the lawn
before heading back to the nest to feed her hungry young
a rabbit sits in silence at the bottom of a tree
shining eyes and twitching nose, I wonder what he makes of me

a cat rubs up against your leg to let you know he's there
he's spent all night on patrol, protecting his rightful lair
the droning of a bumble bee as he goes buzzing by
working flower to flower, collecting nectar for his hive

shadows grow as the sun sinks low and gets swallowed by the sea
fireflies dance in fading light neath the branches of tree
as daylight fades to twilight and twilight turns to night
a self-conscious moon shows itself and bathes the earth in light

by Dawson Stafford

Keith Trayling

I'm married with three grown children and live in Somerset with my wife. I was diagnosed with PD in summer of 2018 (67 years old) and, like all of us, learning to cope with it. On the bright side I have become more creative and immerse myself in writing poetry and reading others. Meeting this group of likewise souls has been a real blessing.

Horns of Uncertainty

You're impaled upon the horns of uncertainty
Climbing a wall that can never be scaled,
Surfing a wave you don't want to ride
Bound by ropes that can't be untied,
Navigating a sea you have never before sailed.

Parkinsons: a multitude of symptoms,
Each an adversary you're trying to fight.
All of us different, but also the same
Shakers Utd playing the same game,
But not ninety minutes, there is no respite.

Carry on; there is no other choice.
Keep your head above water and try not to drown.
Sleep if you can, but then there's the dreams
Nightmares and panic and occasional screams.
Wake up and get up but it's getting you down.

Again! Again! Again! and Again!
Each day a challenge and so you begin.
Start the day and hope for the best
First the tedium of trying to get dressed.
On with the fight that you'll never win.

An uninvited guest who won't go away
His company something, I now have to keep.
He won't kill me, but he'll stay to the end
And wearing me down, I just cannot pretend,
So, into the unknown I continue to leap.

by Keith Trayling

Gardeners Delight

The garden is not just a place for you
To sit, relax and enjoy the view,
But a home to a variety of life.
So, where it's overgrown, don't have a moan,
Smile, don't sit with a frown,
As somewhere out there - be happy to share,
It's a beastie's two up and two down.

So don't concrete it over, leave the grass with some clover,
Some wildflowers - a bonus for all.
Some old rotting wood, well - it really just could,
Be an animal's neat pied a terre.
And birds will sing, as they fly on the wing
The garden is somewhere to share.

So, it's certainly not a waste, to give nature some space,
Somewhere it can do its own thing.
As a manicured garden - well, I beg your pardon
What's wrong with a few natural weeds?
And tarmac, and concrete, it might look quite neat,
But not for the birds and the bees.

by Keith Trayling

Lost

A long winding stroll, down a cold and windy beach
To a cafe that was closed, and you were out of reach
An early start on an empty bus, paying a hopeful fare
Each stop watching the people board, but sadly you're not there
A walk at the weekend, on a crowded shopping street
Countless faceless people, none of whom you wish to meet
Stand in a closed shop doorway, watch them passing by
Take a tissue from your pocket, feel a tear fall from your eye
Then around the corner, and coming into view
Is the one you search for, made to be with you
Where have you been, I've been searching low and high
You wag your tail, give me a bark and lick the tear straight from my eye

by Keith Trayling

Darrell Troon

I have never been an avid reader or writer but since my Parkinson's diagnosis in 2014 I have become obsessed with numerous things which were short lived, thanks to adjustments to medication. But poetry has stayed with me, I think it's belonging to a group of people who understand what each other may be feeling in their poems, and a strong sense of community.

Sleep Eludes Me

Sleep eludes me,
I know it's there,
somewhere
Hiding in the darkness,
makes me want to scream and swear
Tomorrow will be a waste land,
dozing in my chair
Fate has delt me a life of naps,
drained of energy, a routine of fatigue.

But when I'm lucky enough to find some zzzzz's,
my sleep is corrupted by vivid dreams
Monsters and evil things fill my head,
but there's only room for two in our bed.
Kicking and punching I see them all off,
now only one remains, my wife to, has fled.

So, an hour here, and an hour there,
seems to be all my brain can spare
Day after day, night after night
A good night's sleep,
Still eludes me.

by Darrell Troon

Winter Awakens

As autumn settles down to sleep
Winter slowly waking peeps
The leaves of gold now swept away
It's winter's time to come and play

First on the list is to shorten the days
Add lots of clouds, then wind and rain
Block out the sunlight
Then chill the air
Underneath dark clear skies of stars
A frozen world is glistening bright
Winter now wide awake
Lays down deep snow upon the ground
The winter's grip will remain
For some bringing beauty
For others, hardship, and pain
At least until the spring returns
And sends winter on its way

by Darrell Troon

Rope

An old length of damp hemp rope
Short in length but strong
Tied tightly, so as not to break
From the bough of an old oak tree
Swinging freely in breeze
On the edge of a raging river
To a child it was just a toy
Swinging out over the water
Then swinging back again
But for the man who tied the knot
It was not a game
He had swung out by his neck
To put an end to his pain.

by Darrell Troon

David Urwin

I have written poetry from my teenage years, but shared barely any of it for decades, though I now love 'performing' my poetry, or simply reading it to an audience. I have (self) published three collections. I was diagnosed with Parkinson's in September 2021; however, I try to remain positive and upbeat writing poetry on a wide range of topics and in a range of styles. I run a 'spoken word' monthly event with my partner, Jackie Biggs, in Cardigan, west Wales, and attend other local poetry events whenever possible.

Where Were You When the Deckchairs Were Washed Away ?

Two deckchairs stand on a stony beach.
In the one sits a half-peeled banana
and a magnifying glass.
In the other sits the British Prime Minister,
who says, 'Love is a phallic diamond, pure carbon;
I want one', over and over, over, and over,
over and over.
'Love is a phallic diamond, pure carbon, I want one.'

They have a banana in their hand;
its peel drips over their wrist.
The horizon bores like a laser
grey sky, grey sea.
They look out to the sea
and so does the banana.
A bicycle bell is clipped to their nose.
Go on, give it a little ring:
ting-a-ling
ting-a-ling
ting-a-ling
A long, green thread of mucus dangles.

Oh, the stripiness of this!
Oh, the stripiness of that!
Oh, the stripiness of everything!

And who are those wounded, hunched figures
emerging from the sea?

by David Urwin

This and That

The wind rises and falls,
strengthens then drops away.
Washing on the line sways,
lifts, billows. The bed sheet flaps
and slaps itself, happy.
The sun disappears, and then re appears.
The coffee is a rich deep brown in the cup.
Flower buds are forming, a profound pulse
forcing a dream of bloom through the stem.
A towel, brown as my coffee, dances on the line,
swirling its skirt at the nonchalant sheet.

Somewhere, unseen, a family has no food to eat,
a state servant tortures a jailed dissident
and a woman lies dying on a dirty street.

by David Urwin

A spot ov bovver wiv vat ole Parkinsonz

so it's autumn, the fall, summer's gone, cloud hunkers down on your shoulders, you gotta shake it off, where's the sun, it's pissing down AGAIN, you want to sleep, you want to sleep, you want to sleep, but haven't had a good night's sleep since some night you can no longer remember and you're shaking, shaking, that involuntary shaking, you're so sick of shaking but we all have our different burdens to bear so substitute your own condition your own problems, mine's Parkinson's, ta very much god,(substitute fate, if you want) but aren't you shaking and crying at what we are doing to the earth and what we do to each other so you put on some music in your living room and dance yeah to Santana's Let The Children Play or Europa (Earth's Cry, Heaven's Smile) (yeah that seems right) and you're gonna dance those blues right outa your head, just you all alone on yes that stripy recycled cotton rug in your living room, Santana's Moonflower album, dance sister dance, feel the rhythm flowing through you, baila mi hermana, doncha just love the Spanish, what's the world coming to, you gotta dance it away or just shake, the sadness, the rage, burn it off, the tears fall, the flames rise, those conga rhythms help, do what's right for you, but don't hurt anybody else and time passes, oh, time passes...

by David Urwin

Joe van Koeverden

I'm Joe, I live in Winnipeg with my wife Andi and retired from a long career in senior and executive positions in government and the hospitality industry. I was diagnosed with Parkinson's disease in my late fifties which cut short my formal career but opened my time for volunteering for a variety of organisations supporting People with Parkinson's on a local, national and international level. My poems are in a variety of Poetry for Parkinson's publications including my own book "Grab the Spark", an inspirational story of my personal journey over 10 years.

A Focus on Life with PD

What is not wrong with my life?
I will continue to live fully.

Perhaps with new limitations,
As to the amount I can push myself.

But no limits on how much
I can love and cherish life itself

Showing gratitude for gifts received.
Paying it forward with deeds of friendship.

I will fill everyday with love and passion,
For what I have, not what I want.

Giving what I can, not what I thought.
Living with acceptance not anticipation

by Joe van Koeverden

Fred's not here....anymore!

Fred loved to garden
but his mobility then,
Had already shrunken.
So, we shared a plot
But didn't talk a lot
As his bad heart
kept us apart.

He lived alone in B404
But had friends to relate
Who kept him up to date.
He, a gentle soul, said many
Would apologize when sick
But, always looking forward
For another time to click.

With no garden plot to share
He lived behind the door of B404.
This year I didn't see Fred till today,
fully dressed on the basement floor he lay.
It was more than some could bare
A homemade noose he did still wear
while losing heat to the stone floor

The police were many
And had procedures to follow
To ensure no foul play
Was part of this day.
Father Leo came to pray
With those of us that chose to stay.
Supporting us in his special way.

Fred will be missed
Like many other seniors
Who pass away on any day
Were they loved enough?
Could we help them more?
The only certainty is that
Fred's not here, anymore.
"Gone" said the note on his door.

by Joe van Koeverden

Medicine of Choice

I sit restless
at the computer
Trying to calm my mind
to a state of peacefulness
to write a poem

I am confused a little
wondering if the poem
Is the prize
or is the writing
the reward?

Is this a dilemma
Akin to the Chicken and egg?
or would the analogy
of the horse and the cart
Be more applicable?

We take lots of meds
To avoid the symptoms
of pd, so perhaps
this is simply just that,
self-administered medication.

Taking this med requires
Stillness in thought & time
To allow the words to flow
Emotions to be released
Muscles become relaxed.

I am a more gentle man
when I have taken
this medication and enjoy
the reward of sharing
my words in our community

by Joe van Koeverden

Julie Walker

I was diagnosed at the age of 44 in 2012 with YOPD, I can't cure Parkinson's but I can raise awareness. I write poems as the Parkinality poet and contribute a regular column to the local newspaper. I hope when people read my writing they feel less alone when dealing with a disease which is so unreliable and makes those living with the condition unpredictable.

Cured (I am not)

Cured, I am not
I am not cured
I am not cured
I am. Not cured.
If I keep saying it
One line after another
I am not cured
Either yes or no
'Cured' is what we want

It stares at me from the chair
The lack of a cure
It stares and stares
I can't
I just
I can't
Wishing believing
Hoping it to be true
It's all about me
It's all about you

Waiting watching
For the moment to be mine
When there is a cure
When there is a time
When normality is free
When normality is now
When we stop talking about you and me
When we look up
Look at the sky
Think and wonder
Why? Why? Why?

Twisting
Thinking
Back to front
Hoping
Praying
That all will be well
That all will be fine

I can't see the future
I can only see the past
When did I run?
When did I come last?

Overtaken
Over run
Over and under
Life used to be fun

But what is it now?
What has it become?
What is life?
What have we become?

We wander through the day
We wander through the life
That we want to live
That we have started to miss

Mistaken identity
Mistaken mistook
Stop giving me that look
That look of yester year
That look of fear
That look
That says a single tear

by Julie Walker

> "We have Parkinson's, Parkinson's doesn't have us"
>
> *Poets - The Wall*